Toward an Integrated Theory of Development:

Economic and Noneconomic Variables in Rural Development

William F. Whyte

and

Lawrence K. Williams

ILR Paperback No. 5   February 1968

New York State School of Industrial and Labor Relations, a Statutory College of the State University at Cornell University, Ithaca

Price: $1.50

ORDER FROM

Distribution Center, New York State School
of Industrial and Labor Relations,
Cornell University, Ithaca, New York
14850

Contents

·:··:·

On Interdisciplinary
Development Research

"WHILE THE PROGRESS OF THE UNDERDEVELOPED countries depends upon social and psychological as well as economic factors, I would argue that the problems of underdevelopment are basically economic." Thus recently spoke an international expert. But then he went on to say, "By that I mean that the other factors can be expressed in economic terms."

The first statement sounds like nothing more than a standard case of disciplinary imperialism, but then the speaker gives the game away. Of course social and psychological factors can be expressed in economic terms, but economic factors can also be expressed in social and psychological terms. The problem is not to determine which form of expression is correct, but rather to examine the interrelations of economic, social, and psychological variables so as to learn to deal systematically across this conceptual range. Only in this way can a *scientific* theory of development, as against a parochial disciplinary theory, be built.

In this monograph, we tackle only the preliminary task of pointing out some of the interrelations among economic, social, and psychological factors, concentrating upon how economic data may be fitted into the schemes of anthropologists, sociologists, and psychologists. For illustration, we draw upon some research now in progress: "Study of Change in Peruvian Villages." This is a comparative and longitudinal program, with the authors as codirectors for Cornell, with José Matos Mar codirector for the Instituto de Estudios Peruanos in Peru, and with Oscar Alers and Julio Cotler as associate directors. While the cases to be discussed here are nearly all Peruvian, what they illustrate should be equally valid in other parts of the world.[1]

DIFFERENCES IN CASE SIZE

In development research by economists and other social scientists, a major obstacle to conceptual integration is difference in case size. The economist generally focuses his analysis at the level of the nation, the economy as a whole, or some nationwide sector (the agricultural sector, for example). If he comes down from this level, he is hardly content with anything smaller than a region. Sociologists, anthropologists, and psy-

---

[1] A description of the research program is given in the Appendix.

chologists occasionally give attention to the national level, but their studies are more often concentrated on the behavior of particular individuals, groups, organizations, and communities.

As long as each discipline remains at its customary level, the goal of conceptual integration is beyond reach. Only when we all deal with variables in the same case can we determine whether we are talking about the same things under different labels or whether more fundamental conflicts are at issue.

We see little possibility of interdisciplinary theoretical integration at the level of macroeconomics. If we are to exploit the possibilities of such integration at the level of microeconomics, then it is important, not to argue whether economic or social or psychological variables can best explain the development in question, but to look at the joint variance that can be explained by examining an interrelated set of what are conventionally thought of as economic, social, and psychological variables.

Much of this discussion will be focused at the village level, but we shall also be concerned with relating our villages to the surrounding area, to the market towns, and to the structures of economic and political power. Hopefully, somewhere along this pathway from village to nation, it may be possible for economists and other social scientists to get together.

Toward an Integrated Theory

Let us illustrate the translatability of variables in the case of Huayopampa,[2] a Peruvian village in the highlands above the coastal valley of Chancay, which, since 1950, has transformed its economy. From an exclusive reliance upon cattle, corn, potatoes, and other crops traditional to this part of the world, the village has shifted its activities, going heavily into fruit growing.

On the economic side, this change was preceded by a change in, to use the economist's term, "infrastructure": the construction of a road from Huayopampa to the valley, which made it possible to get the new crop to coastal markets rapidly and efficiently. The shift into fruit growing also required the investment of large loans from the Agricultural Development Bank, supplemented by the savings of the villagers. It involved the cultivation of new markets and the importation of new products such as fertilizers,

---

[2] The Huayopampa comments are based primarily upon two documents in the study directed by Dr. José Matos Mar: *San Agustín-Huayopampa: Estructuras Tradicionales y Economía de Mercado,* Fernando Fuenzalida V., Olinda Celestino C., Jurgen Golte R., Teresa Valiente C., and José L. Villarán S., Informe Preliminar, Valle de Chancay, No. 1 (Lima: Universidad Nacional Mayor de San Marcos, with Instituto de Estudios Peruanos and Cornell University, 1966); and Fernando Fuenzalida V., Teresa Valiente C., and José L. Villarán S., *Estructuras Tradicionales y Economía de Mercado: La Comunidad de San Agustín-Huayopampa* (Lima: Universidad Nacional Mayor de San Marcos, Dept. de Antropología, 1967), bachelor's thesis.

insecticides, spray pumps, and other agricultural machinery.

In psychological and social terms, these changes reflect, in part, the psychological phenomenon of deferred gratification. The traditional agricultural cycle had allowed the villagers to reap within a few months the rewards of money and of effort invested. But the fruit trees in question do not begin to yield a crop until five to seven years after planting. The change, therefore, involved not alone an economic decision but a dramatic shift in psychological orientation away from the traditional peasant view — from short-run gratification to deferred gratification in the expectation of greater rewards in the long run. Such a shift does not occur simply because economic analysis indicates the probable availability of such long-run payoffs. There are many cases on record where the apparent availability of long-run payoffs did not bring about the changed behavior. We can only assume that the *perception* of attractive long-range payoffs is a necessary *but not sufficient* condition for inducing villagers to defer their short-run gratifications.

The ways people perceive and evaluate themselves and the world of time, space, activities, and resources strongly influence such economic decisions. In Huayopampa, we found that its particular innovation grew out of a psychological and social context in which education has had an extraordinarily high value (for rural Peru) and in which school teachers have played a role, not only of community leaders, but also of transmission links of technical agricultural knowledge from the Agrarian University and the Ministry of Agriculture to the village farmers. Furthermore, we found that this agricultural shift was but one of a series of innovations in activities and in economic, political, and social organization that our associates have traced back over a period of almost a hundred years. Thus it is that in Huayopampa today nearly any proposed innovation is greeted with a lively interest and openness of mind which stands in marked contrast to that of the other twenty-five villages in our program.

We have already put the road to the valley into the economist's category of infrastructure, but that does not explain how the road came into being. This was no gift from the central government. It came about because Huayopampinos organized themselves and rallied neighboring communities to commit their labor to the project — and then because Huayopampinos were able to exploit already existing ties in Lima to get the engineering studies and the dynamite necessary to make the project feasible.

In an earlier period, Huayopampinos got their corn and potatoes to market on pack animals, but fruit is so bulky and perishable that it could be shipped out only on trucks. At first the villagers consigned their produce to truck owners from other communities. When repeated efforts to get the truckers to lower their "exorbitant" rates failed, Huayopampa established its own communal trucking enterprise. Today most of Huayopampa's agricultural produce is shipped to market in communal trucks or in vehicles owned by individual farmers.

A communal solution to the transport problem depended upon the collective orientation of the Huayopampinos, their organizational skills, and their past successes in cooperative activities, which gave them the confidence to undertake this new enterprise. Our surveys show Huayopampa scoring exceedingly high in collective orientation (the belief that cooperative labor is more effective than individual labor), in faith in people, and in their evaluation of the level of cooperation in their village.

This discussion has not begun to explain the transformation of Huayopampa, but that is not our intention. We use the case simply to illustrate the interrelations of economic and noneconomic variables.

On the Uses and Misuses of Money

When we speak of the uses and misuses of money, we are not seeking to make moral judgments. We are simply noting that some ways of using money contribute to economic growth, some ways have no such effect, some ways may even retard economic growth. It, therefore, becomes important to ask how the rural people use their money, a question seemingly too obvious to mention, yet one to which economists actually give little attention. Many economists seem to assume that, in a country like Peru, there are no financial resources worth considering in the villages and that the problem is one of importing, or creating locally, new sources of wealth.

While the figures on per capita income for rural Peru amply demonstrate the poverty of the area, still, when we sum up the small resources of large numbers of people, we arrive at surprisingly large sums of money, the utilization of which has marked effects on the economic well-being and progress of the villagers. Let us examine, first, some of the unproductive ways in which these funds are used.

INTERGROUP CONFLICT

Enormous sums are used up in rivalries and conflicts between villages, within villages, and between villages and large landowners or *hacendados,* a matter which Ulrich Peter Ritter has examined in his study of "indigenous communities" and cooperatives in Peru. Indigenous communities are villages that have been legally recognized by the national government and have an elected representative, the *personero*, who represents their interests before the Ministry of Labor and Communities in Lima. Although the category was established to include villages that maintain an Indian culture and utilize much of their lands in common, official recognition has been given to any number of villages that can hardly be described as Indian in culture. Furthermore, most of these villages are simply communities of small individual family farms, with what communal land they have being generally limited to grazing areas. There were 4,000 officially recognized indigenous communities in 1965,[3] with hundreds more pressing their claims for such recognition. Since it is estimated that 3,500,000 or 60 percent of the rural population lives in such communities, we are talking about a significant segment of Peruvian rural society. Furthermore, the problems discussed by Ritter seem to be endemic to rural Peru. Here is Ritter's analysis:

> The ambiguous and uncertain situation of communal lands from the legal point of view, on the one hand, and the fanatical devotion of the Indians to these lands they consider their own, give rise to interminable litigations that impoverish the villagers, holding back the development of the economy of the communities and supporting a steadily increasing number of lawyers. Thus it is said that in the last ten years the number of lawyers in Caraz has grown fivefold and in a village as small as Juli [pop. 3874],

---

[3] *Atlas Comunal del Perú*, Lima, 1965.

9

there are now thirty lawyers living off the litigation of the Indians. These court cases sometimes have their origin before the legal recognition of the indigenous community [by the Ministry of Labor and Indigenous Affairs]. Thus the community of Ollantaytambo, Cuzco, has cases that have been in litigation more than forty-four years. We find paradoxical situations such as that of Recuayhuanca, district of Marcará, Ancash, one of the few communities that still has lands that are cultivated in common for the community. There the harvest of these communal lands is divided in the following manner: half to the lawyer, a quarter for the expenses of the *personero,* and a quarter divided among members of the community.

The value of the lands in litigation generally represents only a very small fraction of the sums that are invested in these legal struggles. When the authorities of the community of Huaylas, Ancash, told us that they have been in litigation with a private citizen of the community since the official recognition of the community, the author expected to find this citizen a rich man. He was much surprised when he saw that the man's house was one of the poorest in the village and when the man himself declared that with the money he had invested in litigation over the years, he could have bought an hacienda near Lima. . . .

These litigations appear to the observer like the endless competition of two villages in soccer. One year one village wins, the next year the other, in a contest that never ends. One court decides one way, other courts in another way, but the consequences are more serious than those of athletic contests, for they impoverish both contestants.[4]

How widespread are these legal disputes? On the basis of a mail questionnaire with responses from 754 communities in nine departments, Ritter reports that 653 currently had legal cases in process — over 80 percent. Two hundred thirty-two reported such disputes with haciendas, 237 with other communities, and 184 with private individuals in the communities. The responses came from approximately 40 percent of the indigenous communities to which the questionnaire was sent. We have no way of estimating how representative these figures are but, on the basis of the reports of Ritter and of many other observers, it is safe to say that well over half of the communities of Peru are currently engaged in some sort of land litigation. As Ritter has noted, some of these cases seem to go on forever.

We were first inclined to describe this contest as a zero-sum game in which the gain of one contestant is exactly equal to the loss of the other, and no new resources are created in playing. Such an analogy overlooks the costs involved in playing the game. In the long run, both parties lose, and the only gainers are the lawyers who

---

[4] Ulrich Peter Ritter, *Comunidades Indígenas y Cooperativismo en el Perú*. Ibero-Amerika Institut für Wirtschaftsforschung an der Universität Göttingen. Bilboa, Spain. Ediciones Deusto, 1965, pp. 30–32. Translation by Whyte. The name of the Ministry is now Labor and Communities.

represent them. This fact has not been lost on the legal profession. While doctors are in exceedingly short supply in the rural areas of Peru, we have found no shortage of lawyers who may be appealed to in handling these land disputes. In fact, there seem to be growing numbers of enterprising lawyers who operate like ambulance chasers in our cities. The lawyer will approach the village officials with a sales pitch something like this, "I have been examining the legal records, and I find that your village is not currently enjoying all the lands to which it is entitled because X years ago Y village usurped some of your lands to which they had no legal right. Now, if you would like me to handle the case...."

Important as the financial costs of these contests are, we must not overlook the cost in intravillage and intervillage conflict and mistrust. Our studies in cities as well as in the countryside have shown a general tendency in Peruvian society not to trust your fellow man, and here we see on the rural scene how the sentiment persists and grows.[5]

Intervillage conflict may have no significance for some types of economic activities, but for those which can only be successful if two or more villages work together, the atmosphere of friction and mistrust is obviously a major obstacle to

---

[5] Whyte, "Culture, Industrial Relations and Economic Growth: The Case of Peru," *Industrial and Labor Relations Review,* Vol. 6, No. 4, (July 1963) pp. 583–594.

progress. For example, when the community of Huayopampa purchased a bus and established a regular service from Huayopampa to the valley city of Huaral, the village council recognized that the enterprise would be more successful if the passengers were not limited to residents of their own community. To attract customers from other villages, the authorities in Huayopampa had to establish a schedule of fines for Huayopampinos who insulted non-Huayopampinos on the bus and an even heavier set of sanctions for Huayopampinos who could not resist the temptation to express their feelings physically. While the residents of other communities now travel unmolested on the Huayopampa buses, the strenuous measures taken by the Huayopampa village fathers are evidence of the magnitude of the problem. Furthermore, we should note that very few villages in Peru have a community government as powerful as that of Huayopampa in enforcing the sanctions necessary to overcome the manifestation of intervillage hostility.

The activities of the *personero* can also be examined from this point of view. Peru is a highly centralized country, both economically and politically. Few villages raise any appreciable sums to pay for community services or for new public works, most of them being highly dependent upon the national government to provide them both with the financing and with the technical assistance they need for local progress. The *personero* is the primary lobbyist for village interests and, to make his efforts the more effective, he is often accompanied in this task by a delegation from the community. Since most governmental decisions of any importance to the village are made in Lima, we find *personeros* and their delegations making trip after trip to the capitol to lobby for the interests of their villages. While the villagers do not travel in the style of visiting social scientists or Peruvian professional men, nevertheless these trips do cost money. In fact the *gastos de representación* (costs of representation) are a standard item and often a large one in village budgets. For example, Pacaraos,[6] a less developed village in the neighborhood of Huayopampa, in 1963 spent almost 13 percent of its budget on *gastos de representación* and an additional 3 percent entertaining visiting dignitaries.

It is not alone social scientists who note the economic losses involved in such activities. One of the community leaders of Huayopampa put

---

[6] The Pacaraos comments are based upon several documents in the study directed by Dr. José Matos Mar: Emilio Mendizabal Losack, *Pacaraos: Una Comunidad en la Parte Alta del Valle de Chancay* (Lima: Universidad Nacional Mayor de San Marcos, Dept. de Antropología, 1964); Rodrigo Montoya, *Emigración de una Comunidad Campesina de la Sierra Peruana: Pacaraos* (Lima: Universidad Nacional Mayor de San Marcos, Dept. de Antropología, 1965) bachelor's thesis. Especially helpful has been the study, in preliminary report form at this writing, by Jurgen Golte, Carlos Degregori, Modesto Gálvez, and Jaime Urrutia.

it this way to us, in describing an earlier community project:

> Over a period of fifteen years we sent delega-
> tion after delegation to Lima to try to get the
> government to provide us with the material and
> the technical knowledge we needed to carry out
> the project. This was a very frustrating experi-
> ence because we were always getting promises
> and no action. Besides, when we came back and
> nothing happened, there were always people in
> the community saying that we had just spent
> their money to have a good time in Lima. Finally,
> after fifteen years the government did provide
> the material and the engineering help we
> needed so we could complete the project. But
> then we sat down and figured out how much it
> cost us in expenses for those trips to Lima over
> the years, and we realized that we would have
> got the job done much faster and cheaper if we
> just had bought the materials and hired the
> engineer ourselves.

It is interesting to note that the Huayopampino
recognizes the social and psychological as well as
economic costs of the *gastos de representación.*
The dependence of village leaders upon the government in Lima not only brings them personal
frustrations but stirs up friction and mistrust
within the village.

While it is not our purpose to present solutions
to any of these problems, if we consider certain
action implications, we can explore further the
interrelations of economic and noneconomic variables.

15

Toward an Integrated Theory

The prevalence of land litigation in the rural areas is based in part upon the vagueness and the ambiguities in the laws and in the legal records concerning land in Peru. Where uncertainty prevails, a lawyer can always make some sort of a case for one or the other party in a land dispute. Since this situation has been recognized as a problem in Peru for many decades, we might ask why so little has been done to clarify land titles and to put an end to the disputes. We suspect that such fundamental changes have not been introduced because in the past the vagueness and ambiguity of the land titles worked to the advantage of the wealthy and politically powerful landholders. There are many well-documented cases in which such an individual has extended his holdings through litigations, backed by family connections, the use of money, and the use of force or threats of force. Now, under the pressure of population increases in the villages and the growth of militant peasant organizations, this situation seems to be changing. In the last few years, hardly a day has gone by without a Lima newspaper running a story about what the landlord calls an "invasion" by the peasants and what the peasants call "recovery of our lands that were usurped."

Problems of this nature certainly will not be resolved simply through clarification of existing land titles. Any land reform worthy of the name would necessarily require some sort of redistribution of ownership but, in the process, let us not overlook the legal and economic questions that are involved in land litigation.

If it were possible to bring an end to land litigation in rural Peru, very substantial sums of money would, over the years, become available for productive use. The economic advantages of such a change are as obvious to the villagers as they are to us, but the problem can never be solved in economic terms alone. The economic changes could only come about through legal–political activities. If the necessary political backing were available, we can imagine area-by-area studies aimed at arriving at a firm determination of legal rights to land. Such studies would not in themselves, of course, bring an end to disputes, but we can imagine the creation of some sort of new institution designed to adjudicate land disputes in such a way that the villagers would no longer have to invest such substantial sums in these cases as they do now and so that, hopefully, a case once decided would not continue to appear in the legal system. In other words, changes in the investment of money would have to be brought about through changes in the po-litico–legal system.

The same general point can be made about the *gastos de representación*. As long as Peru is highly centralized politically and as long as local governmental units have neither the autonomy nor the taxing power to meet at least a part of local needs themselves, we can expect the continued draining off of immense sums of money from local communities to finance the sending of individuals and delegations to Lima. In a later section we take up the question of local taxation.

CONSPICUOUS CONSUMPTION IN THE FIESTA SYSTEM

The fiesta system represents another case of apparent misuse of money, from the standpoint of economic development. Each village has its patron saint who must receive his annual communal celebration. Nor is it just the saint's day that is generally celebrated; most fiestas go on for several days. Furthermore, many villages have several saints to whom they pay tribute, which has led some anthropologists to refer to the "fiesta-siesta culture." For thousands of villages, these fiestas represent an enormous investment of scarce resources and also the draining off of labor from productive pursuits.

It is customary, even among anthropologists, to look upon the fiesta as a negative influence on economic progress. Indeed, more detailed studies would probably show this effect in most cases, but the economic outcomes are not so simple as they seem. Let us explore some of their ramifications.

One effect of the fiesta system is to stimulate migration out of the communities. In the highland village of Pacaraos, whose outmigrants have been studied by Rodrigo Montoya,[7] we find many of them explaining that they left in part to escape the burdens that would have fallen upon them if they had remained in Pacaraos and assumed the fiesta obligations of a *comunero* there. Is this a good thing from an economic standpoint? Laughlin Currie[8] would argue that it is, since he holds that the economic advance of Latin American countries depends upon a more rapid pace of industrialization and urbanization than now prevails. However, the current pace of cityward migration in Peru seems to be running well ahead of the capacity of industry to absorb the population, thus creating serious social and economic problems in and around the cities. From the local standpoint, the outward migration may be beneficial in reducing the pressure of population upon the land. On the other hand, the migrants are disproportionately young people and may in some cases be the most active and energetic individuals in the population. If there are indeed economic potentials to some of these villages that could be developed, the loss of such active people may have a severely depressing effect.

While the fiesta, in general, serves to stimulate emigration from the villages, it also serves to

---

[7] *ibid.*

[8] Paper for Conference on the Development of Highland Communities in Latin America, Cornell Latin American Year, 1966.

bring former residents back to the "old hometown" for visits. The close ties maintained between residents and former residents of Peruvian villages are noteworthy. In Lima there are thousands of clubs tying together the former residents of this village or that, and the clubs serve as important links between the city and the countryside. In many cases, the city club raises money to help the hometown. Since the fiesta lures back to the village many more former residents than those who come on any other occasion, one would think that the fiesta in this way would have a modernizing influence — that it would draw the village closer to urban influences and would bring into the village needed resources for making advances.

At the same time, we have to ask what it is that the city club of former residents contributes to the village. In describing the village of Carcas in Ancash, Hernán Castillo[9] paints a most depressing picture of abject poverty and economic stagnation. He notes also that the people of Carcas have only one thing that they are proud of: their fiestas. They fully recognize the ruinous costs of their fiesta system, but they take pride in the fact that their fiestas are known in the surrounding area as being more attractive and elaborate than those put on by other villages. When Castillo looked up the club of former residents in Lima,

---

[9] H. Castillo, T. Castillo, Y. A. Revilla, *Carcas: La Comunidad Olvidada* (Lima: Editorial Estudios Andinos, 1965).

he found them engaged in a project to raise money for Carcas. The anthropologist was appalled to discover that the club intended to make Carcas a gift of a statue of another saint, which would then obligate the village to put on *another* fiesta. The motivation was understandable. The former villagers were devoted to their hometown and, if their gift provided them with another excuse for making those return visits, so much the better. To what effect we have not heard, the anthropologist tried to persuade the club members that another saint was the last thing that Carcas needed and that they might better put the money into buying desks for the village school or in meeting some other more concrete need.

The fiesta might be expected to have some effect upon the internal cohesion of the village, and this in turn might be related to economic advance. At least, if new projects arose which depended upon a cohesive organization to carry them out, such cohesion could be an asset. High cohesion and high productivity do not necessarily go together within the village any more than they do within the factory for, from an economic standpoint, disorganized movement would be better than collective stagnation. It does not necessarily follow, however, that the fiesta is a force favorable to village cohesion. It clearly falls in that category which anthropologists call a "rite of intensification," in which by celebrating their saint the villagers dramatize their collective unity. On the other hand, fiestas tend to involve a large amount of drinking, drunken brawls are common, and one wonders whether the scars from these excesses undermine the cohesion that may be stimulated by collective participation in a folk–religious rite.

The fiesta may strain the social fabric of the community in still another way. In few villages do volunteers step forward to assume the costly obligations of religious leadership. It often takes extreme social pressure to get an individual to serve. Could this lead to resentments and friction?

Yet it appears that some fiestas have a high economic payoff in that they attract visitors beyond former members of the community. While such community fiestas run for outsiders are currently rare, one can imagine that, with increased tourism, some villages will be doing a very nice "fiesta business."

But, in this discussion, we are seeking to raise, not necessarily to answer, questions. Our main conclusions regarding fiestas is that their economic impact cannot be assessed on a global basis. We must first get down to cases and work toward a typology. Eventually we might come out with conclusions of this nature: fiesta type A, under conditions XYZ, will contribute to economic progress. Fiesta type B, under conditions UVW, will tend to hold back economic progress. Our problem would then be to determine the types (probably more than two) of fiestas and also to find the conditions which, in combination with a given type, lead to the economic outcome.

This suggests a new approach to the study of fiestas, in which economic and social data are effectively combined. We need first better records on the costs of fiestas, both in cash and in goods. We need also to know whether the manpower devoted to the activity is indeed labor drawn off from some potentially more productive enterprise or whether the fiesta is carried out in a season when the villagers have little to do that would have economic value. In increasing numbers of cases, anthropologists are reporting the costs of fiestas, at least in money terms, but little has as yet been done to relate these costs to the other economic activities of the community.

We need also to examine the structure of the fiesta system in economic and social terms. In some villages, the main costs fall upon an individual *mayordomo* or *depositario*; in other villages, the burden is shared collectively, and there are many variations in between. It may be that a collectively shared enterprise is more likely to keep the costs within bounds than one in which the pressures fall on the individual responsible. When one person is responsible, he recognizes that his standing in the community depends to some extent upon his ability to put on a show at least as elaborate as that of his predecessors. In many cases the fiesta seems to work something like the potlatch system of the Kwakiutl North

American Indian, wherein the limited economic goods of the community are redistributed by making that individual who has accumulated the most goods be responsible for the fiesta.

We need to know much more than we generally do regarding the sources of the money spent in the fiesta. For example, when it is the responsibility of the individual, we may expect that he will call upon his relatives to help him out, but we want to know who contributes what — and also with what expectation of return. Clearly an exchange is involved. It seems that the individual can never get out of the system except by leaving the community. After he has put on the fiesta himself, depending upon the help of relatives and friends, he becomes obligated to help them when it is their turn.

Our study of Pacaraos has shown that many villagers have spent a number of years working in the mines away from the community. They thus accumulated savings so that when they returned to Pacaraos they would be able to reestablish themselves in the community and assume the obligations of *depositario.*

Also in Pacaraos we found that money was sometimes raised by selling cattle or land. Such sales would generally be made to other members of the community — but not just any other member. We found a small number of relatively well-to-do families, who were devoted supporters of the fiesta system, and who stood ready to provide the necessary cash in return for the cattle or lands of their less prosperous villagers. These exchanges, of course, contribute further to inequality in the economic system of the village.

The absolute cost of the fiesta in a given village is not a very meaningful figure. It is more important to know how this cost relates to the income level of the village. For example, our research associates report that the costs to the *depositario* of the chief fiestas in Pacaraos and Huayopampa were approximately the same: 7,000 soles (about $260 in 1966). We find this amount a very heavy burden in Pacaraos, while in Huayopampa the general income level is so much higher that many individuals can assume that obligation without undue strain — in fact, there is lively competition for the honor of sponsoring a fiesta.

We must also consider the relation of the fiesta to the political system of the community. In some villages, the two systems are more or less separated, whereas in many villages they are closely linked in the sense that only individuals who have passed through various religious *cargos* (offices) are eligible to hold office in the communal government. We suspect that a separation of the two systems may be important for economic progress and also for political development. When the two systems are interlinked in the traditional fashion, political office is, like religious office, looked upon as a man's obligation to the community. Since it takes a long time to accumulate the resources necessary to pass through the various religious *cargos,* political leadership tends to be limited to the older men, who in general will be more traditionally minded. Furthermore, in such a system of automatic progression through traditional pathways, we cannot expect much discussion about the qualifications of a candidate for political office. Such a combined system thus tends to eliminate the possibly stimulating effects of political competition and discussion.

Linking the Village to Urban Markets

It has often been said that millions of Peruvian villagers live largely outside the national economy. Such a statement is misleading. What is really meant is that they do not participate in the market in a manner familiar to economists. They are nevertheless engaged in an exchange of goods and services, and it is important for students of rural development to understand this sector of the economic system.

In the first place, we must recognize that the nature of the economic exchanges involved depends very much upon the distribution of political power. In our program, the most extreme condition of inequality is that found in the Department of Cuzco,[10] where our six Indian communities have traditionally been dominated by the village of Pisaq. While a majority of the villagers of Pisaq would be classified as Indians, the real power figures are the upper-class mestizos, particularly those who own the large haciendas in the area or are related to such landowners. In between the two segments is a transitional group of *cholos* who seem to prey upon the Indians.

The coercive nature of exchanges is the most salient economic feature of this situation. When Indians come to Pisaq on Sunday market day, they are met on the road outside the village by the *alcanzadores*. The term comes from the verb, *alcanzar*, which means "to catch up to, to overtake; to reach; to grasp." We might say that this is sort of an out-reach program which saves the Indians the time and trouble of selling the goods themselves in the Pisaq market. The *alcanzadores* take the produce away from them at prices established by the *alcanzadores*. If the Indians refuse to sell at the prices dictated, they are beaten up, and the produce is taken away from them anyway.

There is also a system of requisitioning. The mestizo picks out a chicken, pig, or other animal owned by an Indian, pays the Indian the price

---

[10] Our studies in Cuzco have been under the direction of Dr. Oscar Nunez del Prado. For the material on Pisaq, the mestizo community, we are particularly indebted to the work of Angel F. Garméndia. For our data on the hacienda of Chawaytiri, we are indebted to Thomas Cevallus.

dictated by the mestizo, and goes off with the goods.

In the traditional situation, the Indian is afraid to demand his right to keep the animal or even to get a price he considers fair. Furthermore, there seems to be a customary price established among the mestizos for a given animal or fowl. We have the impression that these prices have remained at the same traditional level for a number of years. This is one way mestizos have of beating the rising cost of living.

In the past, in coming to Pisaq to make purchases, the Indians have been subjected to a system of enforced barter. Certain storekeepers would not allow the Indian to purchase for cash. They insisted instead that he trade his eggs or chicken or some other produce in return for what he wanted to buy. By establishing the values involved on both sides of the barter, the storekeeper could buy the Indian's produce for a fraction of its value in the local market or, to look at it on the other side, could sell products to the Indian at several times their cash price.

It is interesting to note that this system of enforced barter has recently been abandoned in Pisaq, in reaction to the establishment of a co-operative store in one of the Indian villages, promoted by the applied anthropology program directed by Dr. Oscar Nuñez del Prado. Here we have an interesting case where the introduction of competition has brought an abrupt change in certain economic exchanges in Pisaq.

The villages in our other areas of study are not subjected to such coercive controls on their buying and selling. Nevertheless, it would be unrealistic to think of them in relation to the classic economic conception of the free and competitive market. At least, the villagers do not seem to regard these urban markets as either free or competitive. They have a picture of an organized system designed to rig the prices for goods and for transportation to the market to their disadvantage. With only the fragmentary data we have at hand, it is impossible to say how much of this is folklore and how much is real.

These matters will remain in the field of conjecture until we can interest research men in following the produce from the village step-by-step through transportation, through wholesale and retail channels, to the ultimate consumer, examining the prices charged and services performed at each step.

Such studies of economic transactions must be placed in the context of social structure and political power. The middleman is often looked upon as a parasite. In many of the situations we have observed, the middleman performs essential functions. What is in question is the value he receives in return for the services he performs. We would not expect this equation to be determined primarily by the character and personality of the middleman. We would hypothesize a relationship between the relative advantage received by the middleman and the nature of the social structure and distribution of political power in the area where producer and middleman meet. In an "open" area, where social class lines are not sharply drawn, where communities enjoy some autonomy, and where political influence is widely distributed, we can expect the profits of the middleman to be relatively low. In an area where social class lines are dominated by outside power figures, and where political power is highly concentrated (assuming that the producer is at the bottom of this structure), we can expect the profits of the middleman to be relatively high.

On the buying side in the village, we can be much more confident in our description of the situation. In the United States we do not worry about the problem of getting supplies to the farmer. We assume that the local dealer will have in stock what the farmer needs, or, if he does not, he can get it delivered in a short time. Such is not the case in Peru or in other developing countries.[11] It is easy to document cases where farmers

---

[11] This condition is apparently widespread. In "Rural Development in Eastern Nigeria" (the Ford Foundation, 1966, mimeo.), David R. Smock writes, "Very often promotional campaigns are more successful than supply programs and farmers are understandably disappointed when they do not receive the seeds, or seedlings and other materials they have been led to expect."

have not been able to get the fertilizer or other agricultural supplies for which they were prepared to pay. Also common are cases where the necessary supplies arrived too late to do any good. Furthermore, there is the very troublesome problem of coordinating the item to be purchased with the technical information necessary to use it effectively. For example, the agricultural extension agent tells the farmers about the insecticide they should be using and tells them how to use it. But he does not bring any of the product along with him, nor is it locally available. Thus he is unable to demonstrate how it should be used. When the product finally does arrive, the extension agent is nowhere to be found. A few adventurous farmers buy the insecticide, but some of them use it so heavily as to damage the plants and raise their spraying costs, while others use it so lightly that it can have no constructive effect.

The most salient feature of this buying and utilization process is its unpredictability — an aspect upon which we elaborate in a theoretical discussion in a later section.

The linking of the village to the urban market is a problem area that has been given very little attention by agricultural economists. To be sure, there have been a number of useful studies made of urban agricultural markets, but they do not meet two important needs that we see in the type of study we have in mind. In the market itself, the economist tends to formulate his problem in normative terms. He evaluates the efficiency of the market to assess whether the spread between the price paid to producers and the price charged to consumers is excessive. The economist may be aware that the price at each point is not a purely economic phenomenon but is also affected by the structure of interpersonal relationships linking the village to the market, but he has no conceptual tools for dealing with such problems of social organization. Furthermore, he tends to concentrate his attention on the city market itself and rarely traces back step by step the links that bind the village to the market, in order to examine the effects of the market system on the economic progress of particular villages. We badly need socioeconomic studies of this set of organized relationships.

Anthropologists and sociologists who focus their attention on villages do indeed note some of the economic phenomena described here, but in the ordinary field report we find fragmentary information about buying and selling scattered through pages of discussions of political power, the religious system, family organization, and so on. Furthermore, the anthropologist or sociologist is not inclined to be much concerned about costs and other economic values. He is satisfied when he points out that the mestizo buys a pig from an Indian at a fraction of its market value and that the Indian is powerless to reject the transaction.

While this is important information, an adequate economic analysis would involve providing information on the price paid for this pig in relation to the prices received by big producers who were not forced to sell in this way in the general area. We would also want to know how often such transactions take place, so that we could assess the impact upon the economy of the Indians — and of the mestizos.

Of course, it is not easy to get such figures together, but it will only be done when agricultural economists or behavioral scientists with an interest in economic aspects recognize the importance of such documentation. Even then, as we measure the direct economic costs of exploitation of oppressed people, the indirect costs will escape measurement. We can measure the direct loss to the Indian on the forced sale of his pig, but we cannot measure how many more pigs he would raise and sell if he were not faced with the fear and uncertainties involved in the exploitative relationship.

Local Taxation and Public Works

In the past, Peruvian villages have had only minimal powers to levy local taxes. It has been the national government that has levied and collected taxes, the local communities then being dependent upon the money that they can persuade the national government to put at their disposal.

This adequately describes the general situation in money terms, but it overlooks what we might call a labor tax. In many communities we find a traditional system known as the *faena* of communal labor. The village authorities determine the work that is to be done. Instead of levying taxes in money upon the property owners to pay for the work, in effect they tax the community in labor to be contributed by the householders toward the project. It is in this way that much of the maintenance and improvement of Peruvian villages get carried out.

While the system is widespread in rural Peru, how it operates may vary from area to area, particularly in response to the distribution of political power. For example, in the Mantaro Valley[12] where the villages are reasonably autonomous and there are no large landowners dominating the area, the system works in a genuinely democratic fashion to get villagers to contribute their labor toward projects in the selection of which they and their elected representatives have an important voice. In other areas of indigenous communities dominated by large *hacendados* and

---

[12] Our studies in the Mantaro Valley have been under the direction of Gabriel Escobar, Juan Elías Flores, and Oscar Gonzalez. See also Richard N. Adams, *A Community in the Andes: Problems and Progress in Muquiyauyo* (Seattle: University of Washington Press, 1959).

mestizo officials, in practice the *faena* has been a system whereby the mestizo authorities have conscripted labor to take care of work projects selected entirely by the mestizo authorities.

At least in those areas where the *faena* can be considered a voluntary democratic institution, community development experts tend to look upon it as providing a great source of strength for progress. Since the community has the tradition and capacity of mobilizing itself to get work done, the addition of technical knowledge and materials not locally available may serve to create wealth that would not otherwise come into being.

While these resources do, indeed, serve community development efforts, we should not overlook the political and economic hazard that has been pointed out by sociologist James Green[13] of A.I.D. He notes that many projects, which can be carried out in the flush of enthusiasm of contributed labor and technical assistance and materials, carry an obligation to assume the cost of maintenance and repair, if such projects are not to deteriorate. Thus it is quite possible for a national government which has a highly successful community development program to build up an enormous load of maintenance and repair costs for which the villagers cannot or will not tax themselves and which would be too much for the national government to support in the future.

---

[13] Personal conversation.

Is there no way out of this impasse? An interesting experiment along this line is now going forward in Peru under the name of the Revolving Community Loan Fund. Developed by Dr. Green and his associates, the basic idea is that, where there has been no tradition of local taxation, the villagers cannot be expected to accept local tax rates in general terms. They can only be expected to tax themselves (in "rates," not to be called taxes) in order to support an important project to which they are committed. According to the approach now being taken, when the villagers have a project which requires materials they cannot produce, they can apply to *Cooperación Popular,* the government community development agency, for technical assistance in designing the project and for the necessary materials. They are also expected to commit themselves on the labor that the community will furnish. If *Cooperación Popular* officials judge the project feasible from a technical standpoint, they also estimate the price of the materials that will be required and ask the community leaders whether the villagers are prepared to pay this price over a period of years. Where the local officials are ready to make this commitment in writing, they can apply to a government bank for a loan. The money is not paid directly to them, but it is up to them to get bids on the materials and to present the bills of the successful bidder to the bank for payment, when the village authorities are

satisfied that the materials in the proper amount
and quality have been furnished. Over the years
then, the loan is repaid through what are, in
effect, taxes, although the wording of the agreement is careful to avoid the word "taxes." The
villagers are also required to make a formal commitment to provide labor and funds for upkeep
of the project before it can be authorized.

Here we see an ingenious combination of a
social and organizational strategy to achieve the
economic result of levying local taxes and stimulating economic improvements. It is the hope of
the sponsors of the plan that, once the villagers
get used to connecting their payments with particular improvements, in the long run they will
get used to the idea of regular taxation.

Organization and the Price of Labor

The traditional hacienda system of the Peruvian sierra has long been the target of social
critics and is coming under increasing social and
political pressures. There seem to be two main
directions that change can take. One would be
land reform whereby the *colonos* gain title to the
land which they have been working for the
hacendado. The other route could be a peasant
movement, in effect unionizing the *colonos* and
establishing bargaining relations with the land-

owners. Of course, these two routes are not mutually exclusive. With increasing political pressures, the bargaining relationship might be transformed into peasant ownership.

Land reform clearly involves a combination of economic, political, and social organizational aspects. It is the organizational aspects on the countryside that are likely to be overlooked both by the traditional political scientist and the orthodox economist. It has often been said that the Peruvian agrarian reform law is "weak," and from this observation is drawn the conclusion that not much "reform" on the countryside is to be expected. Such a prediction is unlikely to be trustworthy unless we consider the conditions of political and social organizations. If the law is "weak" but the peasants are well organized and militant and have some political support, we can expect more change than would occur with a much "stronger" law without effective peasant organization. In other words, we must learn to think in terms of a combination of variables.

The same sorts of combinations must be put together as we examine the other probable route of rural development through unionization.

Let us first provide some general background on the traditional sierra hacienda. While there are many variations, the type usually includes the following features. Land is controlled by an owner or renter, and the Indians have rights to cultivate their own small plots (generally in the most disadvantageous areas) only as long as they comply with the obligations imposed by the *hacendado*. The Indians resemble European serfs in the manor of the middle ages, the main difference being that the Indian is free to leave the hacienda — but in so doing he gives up any rights to the land he has been cultivating.

For the right to cultivate his small plot, the Indian family head must provide three or four days a week of work under the direction of the *hacendado*. The work may be done on the land of the *hacendado*, but he also may contract out his Indians to others who have work to be done, in which case payment is to the *hacendado* and not to the Indian. Each Indian household is responsible for providing certain personal services in the household of the *hacendado* and for making certain contributions in animals and fowl. Furthermore the requisitioning system we have noted in the indigenous communities of Cuzco is to be found on the hacienda, the *hacendado* or any of his employees being free to requisition an animal or fowl from an Indian family and make a traditional form of payment, generally far less than what would be the market value.

Such Indians traditionally receive a small daily supply of coca to chew and a nominal money payment. Not long before we began our study of the hacienda of Chawaytiri[14] (near Pisaq in

---

[14] Chawaytiri report, *op. cit.*

Cuzco), the Indian *colonos* were receiving one sol (less than four cents) daily.

As part of a general peasant movement that was spreading through the Department of Cuzco, hacienda Chawaytiri became unionized. After an extended legal, economic, and political struggle, the *hacendado* was forced to negotiate an agreement with his unionized Indians. The contract contained a long string of points on wages and working conditions, that sound familiar to the student of collective bargaining. The number of days to be worked was drastically reduced. Personal service obligations to the *hacendado's* household were eliminated. Indians could work in his household only if they voluntarily chose to do so in return for a money wage. The practice of requisitioning animals and fowls from the Indians was eliminated. The daily work payment was raised from one to three soles.

The contract also called upon the *hacendado* to fire his administrator. While this step was not carried out, the Indians reported a marked change for the better in relations between themselves and the administrator and other supervisory personnel.

The peasant movement, of which the Chawaytiri unionization was a part, also included so called "invasions" of hacienda lands in other parts of Cuzco. These movements led to a strong conservative reaction against the Belaúnde Government, which brought about the downfall of his Minister of Government who was responsible for maintenance of law and order. The succeeding Minister of Government ordered a round up of allegedly Communist agitators in the Cuzco area, and the chief union leaders were put in jail. This led to the disappearance of the union at Chawaytiri as a formal organization. It is interesting to note that the situation at Chawaytiri nevertheless did not revert to the *status quo ante.* While the *hacendado* and his administrative staff managed to regain some of the privileges they had lost, they were unwilling to risk the effort to increase the number of days of work obligation. The Indians reported that they were still treated with much more consideration by their supervisors than was the case before unionization.

At one point the *hacendado* announced that, since business was poor, he could no longer pay three soles a day to his workers and that the rate would go back to one sol. This move was greeted by a strike. no work at all for the *hacendado* until payment went back to three soles.

The conflict was settled when the *hacendado* agreed to reinstate the three soles payment. Dr. Oscar Nuñez del Prado reports that one factor in this decision was the *hacendado's* discovery that his lands might have some possibilies for mining. In that case, an assured and reasonably docile labor supply became suddenly much more important to him.

We have presented simply the bare outlines

of the case in order to illustrate how its analysis might be approached. We can look at the relationship between the *hacendado* and the Indians in terms of economic exchanges of goods and services. While we can call the preorganization situation one of human exploitation, this represents a moral judgment and does not provide us the tools for analysis. Disadvantageous as the exchange appeared to the Indians, we can nevertheless discover, describe, and to a large extent measure the elements that went into the exchange between the *hacendado* and his Indians.

How do such exchange relations change? One possible route is through organization. As the peasants organize and the structure of interpersonal relations changes, the balance of the elements in the economic exchange also changes. In analyzing such a situation, we must therefore be able to relate economic and social organizational variables.

As the final step in our case indicates, there may be other important forces operating. Here the *hacendado* got a new conception of the economic activities in which he might engage. This new conception, concerning his mining enterprise, also changed his conception of the prices he was willing to pay for the services he required. This note regarding the birth of "economic man *hacendado*" leads us into consideration of the *hacendado* and the spirit of maximization.

The Hacendado *and the Spirit of Maximization*

According to classical economic theory, the man who owns or controls certain resources is expected to behave in such a way as to maximize his returns from those resources. There are haciendas to which the theory seems to apply reasonably well, and there are others in Peru to which it does not seem to apply at all. By and large, economic man seems to be in control in the coastal haciendas, which are devoted to large-scale production of cotton, sugar cane, and citrus fruits. Many of these haciendas are highly mechanized, and agronomists and agricultural engineers apply the latest scientific methods to the farm enterprise. The workers are paid wages, and, in many cases, they are represented by unions which bargain on wage rates and working conditions for them.

Few economic men are found among the *hacendados* of the sierra. The traditional *hacendado* seems to be less concerned with maximizing the returns from the hacienda than with minimizing his investments in it. In the sierra, the *hacendado* tends to be an important man socially and politically, and he seems to look upon his base in land ownership or control more in terms of what it will do to protect or enhance his social and political position than in terms of increasing economic returns. While he would like to make more money, he does not see that increasing his financial investments and changing the structure of relations with his work force offer promise of greater economic returns. He is satisfied with what agricultural experts regard as an exceedingly inefficient operation as long as it brings in enough to maintain his customary standard of living.

The incentive for investment is further minimized by the legal, economic, and social conditions surrounding the rental of agricultural property in the sierra. Many of these properties are not owned by individual families. They are the property of the state, the church, or of a public benefit society (which uses its income for the support of hospitals and other charitable activities). According to the prevailing pattern, these haciendas are rented out on ten-year leases on the basis of what is supposed to be competitive bidding.

The economics of this system can only be understood in a social context. We find in many cases that the haciendas go for ridiculously low rentals. In effect, the bidding is neither free nor competitive. The winner is likely to be a relative, close friend, and/or political ally of those who make the decisions on the leases.

This leads to an interesting problem later when such lands may be expropriated in favor of the *colonos,* providing agreement can be reached on compensation to the owners. In a free and competitive system, one would think that the rental actually being paid on a property would seem a reasonable index to the fair purchase price of that property. In a country where bank credit costs 15 percent per year or more (except in certain governmental programs), we might say that a purchase price of between ten and twenty times the annual rental would be very generous to the owner. Cases are on record in Peru where owners have demanded more than five-hundred times the annual rental. In effect, they thus acknowledge that the rental figure has been based much more on social than upon economic values. But if rentals are not used as a guide to purchase prices, this adds to the difficulties land reform authorities face in arriving at reasonable assessments.

The ten-year lease arrangement has negative effects upon the development of such hacienda lands. While the lessor may hope to keep the land throughout his active career, he cannot be sure of maintaining such connections with the owners that he will still have the inside track when his first ten years come to an end. If he makes any investments to improve the land, he also makes it more attractive to competitive bidders and increases the possibility that somebody will outmaneuver him the next time around. Rather than risk losing his investment, the lessor tends to put as little as he can into the land while he tries to squeeze as much as he can out of land and people.

While this is exploitation from the standpoint of the *colonos* and social critics, it is not generally a very profitable enterprise for the lessor of the land. For example, at the time Allan R. Holmberg bought out the lease on hacienda Vicos for Cornell University, the former lessor claimed that he was losing money although he was paying less than $1,000 per year to rent 40,000 acres and approximately 1,700 Indians.

When Vicos was expropriated in favor of the Indians in 1962 (five years after expropriation had been guaranteed by the Peruvian government), the Indians were able to pay annual installments of between $4,000 and $7,500 out of their agricultural surpluses. How could such a dramatic economic improvement take place? We shall not undertake to retell the Vicos story here. Let us sum up by noting that at Vicos a feudal manor was transformed into a self-governing community, which functioned economically as a producer's cooperative.[15]

---

[15] The critical top-level relationships were worked out between Holmberg, representing Cornell, and Dr. Carlos Monge, then president of the Indigenous Institute of the Ministry of Labor and Indigenous Affairs. William Blanchard worked with Holmberg at Vicos in establishing the program. Dr. Mario Vázquez, Peruvian anthropologist, played a key role at Vicos throughout the entire period. The Vicos story has been told in various publications. See especially, Allan R. Holmberg, Mario C. Vázquez, Paul L. Doughty, J. Oscar Alers, Henry F. Dobyns, and Harold D. Lasswell, "The Vicos Case: Peasant Society in Transition," special issue of *The American Behavioral Scientist*, vol. 8, no. 7 (March 1965).

The case of Vicos should not be interpreted to mean that there are unlimited economic possibilities in the rural sierra, if the problems of social organization can be resolved. There are very real and serious problems of overpopulation in relation to land and of poor quality of land and inadequate supplies of water. Nevertheless, the Vicos case does indicate that reorganization of the structure of human relations and provision of greater incentives for the Indians could provide substantial improvements.

Could these changes come about only through land reform? What would happen if an hacienda were operated by an *hacendado,* modern style, equipped with a knowledge of scientific agriculture, a new conception of the structure of relationships on the farm, and a maximizing spirit?

There are not many but we hear there are several such individuals in the sierra. We hope eventually to include an hacienda of this type in our study program, so as to increase the range of our knowledge of relationships between different structural patterns and economic and social outcomes on the farm.

Such studies would lead us not only into examination of the way the *hacendado* operates to achieve his social and economic results. We would also want to know who he is and how he got that way. The personal background would be important, for such a man (if indeed he exists) would be a marked departure from the traditional culture of the Peruvian sierra. This man would be playing a role that has been previously unknown in that part of the world. We would, therefore, want to know not alone how he plays this role but what in his personal background made him want to play it and has enabled him to play it effectively. Such studies clearly involve linking up the psychological concerns of child development and personality formation with research on social organization and studies of economic activities.

We might find that the new orientation of the modern *hacendado* derives not simply from humane sentiments but from the requirements of directing modern agricultural activities. When all workers are unskilled and the methods of agriculture are highly labor intensive, then one set of workers is perhaps as good as the next. When complex modern technology must be applied and maintained and if exact procedures must be followed, then a reliable, constant, and trained work force is a considerable asset, and the cost of "developing" the peasant has direct economic payoff. While this does not deny the development of more humanitarian values on the part of the modern *hacendado,* it does suggest that, when social conscience and economics have a joint payoff, those who are able to see the long-range implications of one may be able to see the long-range implications of the other.

Furthermore, we should expect changing relations between *hacendado* and peasants to accompany increased differentiation of the social structure of the agricultural enterprise. Comparing the modern coastal hacienda with the traditional sierra hacienda, we are struck by the much greater differentiation and complexity of organization in the coastal type. Not only is the coastal type much more differentiated in levels of skills among blue-collar workers; we also find white-collar employees concerned with record-keeping, payroll, work schedules, and the like. And the top administration consists not only of the owner or administrator but also of several "staff" specialists, concerned with the application of technical knowledge.

In contrast, the typical sierra hacienda, in administrative terms, is a simple line organization. Power and expertise are not differentiated organizationally. The structure is adaptive only for the *controlling* of a simple traditional set of activities and of an undifferentiated work force.

We do not assume that the psychological orientation and administrative skills required for directing a large modern agricultural enterprise will come to the modern *hacendado* automatically as he resolves the economic and agronomic problems of the enterprise. We do assume that success in operating such enterprises will depend upon a combination of cognitive and social abilities that enable the operator to devise an administrative strategy adequate for meeting the social, economic, and agronomic problems of modern agriculture.

To some extent, the development of administrative strategies may be an evolutionary process, with effective adaptations surviving and ineffective ones dropping by the wayside. Thus the *hacendado* who had a modern vision of human relations on the farm but who could not resolve the economic and technical aspects of the enterprise would necessarily fail. By the same logic, the *hacendado* who had a modern view of the economic and technical aspects of the enterprise but who attempted to maintain the simple and rigid authority system of the traditional hacienda would also fail — unless he were able to adapt his administrative methods to the requirements of the new economic and technical system.

Such conclusions are based upon experience and theory in other fields of human activity. To test them and to develop their application to rural populations and enterprises, we need research on varying patterns of organization structure, administrative strategy, and economic and technical activities.

Economic Incentives, Agricultural Activities, and Social Organization

In our discussion so far, we have made casual reference to the question of economic incentives. We assume that economic incentives are important (a point we shall develop further in our theoretical conclusion), but we also assume that incentives will only bring forth the efforts they are designed to produce if they are integrated with particular combinations of agricultural activities and social organization.

It is misleading and unrealistic to conceive of incentives in terms of economic rewards offered directly to a given individual in response to the personal effort and financial investment that he puts forth. This conception applies to some situations but not to others. Let us attempt a typology of structural situations through considering different types of improvement projects that might be introduced by change agents. We shall distinguish four main types and present an illustration of each:

1. *Individual Direct.* Here the payoff is to the individual or his family in direct relationship to the investment made by that unit. Such would be the case on an individual family farm where the family tries a new seed, invests in fertilizer, applies insecticide, and so on.

2. *Individual through Group, with Equal Shar-ing.* Here the individual or his family receives the rewards from the completion of a project in which he has participated as a member of a group. For example, the villagers in St. Agustín de Cajas[16] in the Mantaro Valley recently com-pleted a reservoir to provide potable water for their community. The labor was entirely supplied by the community. Each household which had provided the required number of man-days' work received equal access to the water upon comple-tion of the system.

Under most conditions, it is not necessary to mobilize all families in a village in order to carry out a project of general community benefit. If a small minority of families refuses to participate, the project may nevertheless proceed, provided there is some way to penalize the nonparticipants or at least to exclude them from the full benefits of the project. However, some communal projects cannot be successful unless participation is 100 percent or close to that figure. Such a project presents much more formidable problems of com-munity organization than does one which can survive with a number of nonparticipants.

Let us consider such a case from the Philip-pines.[17] The seeds to be introduced by the change

---

[16] For the reports on San Agustín de Cajas, we are indebted to Rosa Mejía.

[17] For this case, we are indebted to Gelia Castillo and Mil-ton Barnett.

agent were expected to yield a richer harvest than before, and the plants would mature at a somewhat different time. But this particular area faced a serious infestation of rats and birds, which set upon crops reaching maturity. As long as all farms came to the harvest period at about the same time, the impact of the pests would be spread so widely that no single farmer would suffer intolerable damage. On the other hand, if one farmer had a field reaching the point of harvest earlier or later than his neighbors, all the rats and birds in the area would converge upon his crop, and he would be ruined. Thus, if the innovation brought the crop in early, it could not be introduced unless it were possible to get nearly all the villagers to change at the same time. This may be impossible in a program that depends entirely upon voluntary cooperation of individual farmers.

A similar problem is presented by programs calling for consolidation of land holdings. In many parts of the world, efficiency of farming is depressed by fragmentation of land ownership. It is not just that the farmer has too little land (though that also may be the case) but that his holdings are scattered in a number of widely separated fragments. This may not be serious if the farmers customarily let some of their fields lie fallow each year and if they do not use farm machinery. But when fertilizers are applied so that each plot is planted every year, then the dispersion of the plots adds enormously to the labor required. Dispersion also greatly reduces the economies possible through the use of machinery.

In some cases, consolidation of land ownership will be needed before the advances of modern agricultural knowledge and technology can be applied. But consolidation calls for inclusive community action. If even a few families refuse to go along with a redistribution of land, they may prevent their fellows from enjoying the benefits of such a program. Here again it may not always be possible to carry out such consolidations purely on a voluntary basis. Some experience suggests that this is a most complex and difficult problem requiring a combination of community participation, economic incentives, and governmental sanctions against holdouts.[18]

Consolidation also involves questions of equity: whether each family is getting a fair equivalent for what it is giving up. While providing an approximate balancing of interests is not inherently impossible, there are always likely to be some villagers who will conclude that the program really falls in the type now to be discussed.

3. *The Differential Impact Project.* In this case, some members of the community stand to gain much more than others through the success of

---

[18] For this analysis, we are indebted to Smock, *op. cit.*, Part I: "Land Fragmentation and the Possibility of Consolidation."

the project, or we may even have a case where some members gain and others lose. In the Vicos community, for example, a reforestation project was recently carried out with large-scale planting of eucalyptus trees.[19] Those who worked on the tree planting received compensation, so there was equal sharing of rewards in this respect. However, the location of the project had a differential impact upon the community, for it eliminated a substantial area of grazing land. This was of no concern to most of the families with only a few head of cattle, but it was a matter of real consequence to several families owning large herds. It is not surprising that opposition to the project was concentrated among these families.

4. *Controlling Individual Interests in Favor of Group Interests.* In such cases, if the community as a whole is to benefit, individual members must be restrained from doing what otherwise would be rewarding to them and their families. Such cases are often found in the field of animal husbandry.

Let us say that the village in question is predominately dependent upon cattle for its economic existence. Let us say further (and this would be a typical case) that the quality of the cattle is low and that the village faces a problem of overgrazing. There are too many cattle for the available pasturage, and the cattle are beginning

---

[19] Personal conversation with Mario Vázquez.

to eat the grass to the roots and destroy the land cover.

From a technical point of view, what needs to be done is clear. A breeding program must be introduced to improve the quality of the cattle. Then, either the available pasturage must be increased or the size of the herd must be reduced. We do not wish to underestimate the technical complexities of such a solution, but let us assume that the appropriate strain of cattle for breeding purposes is available, that the operation can be financed and that adequate technical knowledge is also available.

Let us now look at the "structural incentive" problems involved. A breeding program does not simply require the introduction of new wealth into the community to be effective. Which animals are to be bred with which and which animals are not to be allowed to breed must be established. Here we have to think not only of the control of people but also of animals and of a large area of physical space.

In village cattle culture, the grazing lands are usually communal, not the property of any particular family. The villagers, therefore, have to decide what the particular rules of the development project shall be and how they shall be enforced over a wide area, with moving crops, day and night.

The village also faces a problem of conflict between individual and community payoffs. From the standpoint of the welfare of the community as a whole, it may be important that certain numbers of inferior animals are excluded from the breeding pool, and yet it is in the interest of the owners of these particular animals to breed them with better quality animals.

When we consider the problem of herd limitation, we face an unavoidable and large-scale conflict between individual and community interests. It is in the interests of each individual cattle owner to have as many animals on the range as possible, and yet if each individual owner follows his own immediate interests, the results will be disastrous for the whole community.

We speak of a "structural" approach to incentives, for it is clear that response to incentives can only be interpreted against the structural properties of the innovation. In the first case, that of the individual family farm, no new structural problem is presented. If the individual farmer can be persuaded to try out the innovation and if it then pays off on his land, he will naturally want to continue with the new practice. Furthermore, the practice is likely to enter into the channels of diffusion, as his neighbors observe his success.

In the second case, *Individual through Group, with Equal Sharing*, it is necessary to mobilize a group, but there is little problem in the distribution of rewards, so that execution of the project may serve to strengthen group solidarity.

(As we have noted, whether *all* members of the community must participate makes a good deal of difference in the difficulty of the project.)

In the third case, *Differential Impact,* a built-in conflict exists, and the village must find some way of coping with it.

The fourth case, *Controlling Individual Interests in Favor of Group Interests,* poses the most difficult structural problem of all. To be effective, the organization must include all cattle owners in the community. They must not only participate; they must also submit to control. In such cases, it is probably misleading to think in terms of a cooperative, at least in any usual sense. Unless coercive powers are lodged in the hands of those operating the program, we can expect the individual owners to follow their individual interests. The villagers may have to build — or fit into — a powerful type of organization, with which they have not had previous experience.

Theoretical Integration

Our main effort has been directed at illustrating the interrelations among economic and non-economic variables. To build an integrated theory of rural economic development is a monumental task and far beyond the scope of this monograph or the capacity of its authors. The discussion so far does, nevertheless, lead us to some general theoretical formulations in three problem areas: motivation theory, economic incentives and social organization, and a socioeconomic analysis of exchange.

We regard these three formulations as simply providing preliminary guidelines that may hopefully one day facilitate the more effective integration of economics and the behavioral sciences.

MOTIVATION THEORY

While there is great concern among change agents and theorists of economic development about the motivation of given populations, we feel that much of this thinking is based upon an oversimplified and inadequate notion of the nature of motivation. Furthermore, we suspect that much behavior that is popularly explained in terms of lack of motivation can be more adequately explained in other terms. The lack-of-motivation argument is indeed one of the most popular excuses for failure that is given by frustrated change agents. If they can say that the people in question really were determined to stick with their traditional way of doing things and did not want to improve their lot, then the blame for failure can be shifted from the change agent to the population.

This way of thinking focusses attention on the question: What do people want? We feel that this question is of dubious value. In remote tribes, isolated from urban life, people may not be aware of the "advantages" of modern urban civilization, and we can therefore say that they do not want some of the features of this civilization, but this characterization would probably hold for only a small fraction of the world's population. It is certainly not true for those parts of rural Peru that we have studied. Even in the most isolated areas, whereas the people may not hunger after television, they do want radios — and transistor radios in large numbers have reached out into the countryside far beyond the extension of electric power. We find widespread dissatisfaction with their lot among rural people and, when we ask them what the most important improvements for their villages would be, we come back with answers that seem well in line with what outside experts themselves would say the villagers need. High on the list are schools and general educational improvements, more land and better irrigation systems, potable water, improvements in medical facilities, and so on. Even technical assistance for agriculture receives a respectable number of votes.

These people certainly want change and what we would regard as improvement. Are they then motivated? That depends upon our conception of the nature of motivation. To speak meaningfully of motivation, we must consider not a single aspect, but at least four: The goals toward which efforts are to be directed; anticipated costs of reaching a given goal, in relation to anticipated rewards of reaching the goal; perception of the probabilities or odds of reaching a given goal; anticipated time span between first effort for the given goal and the payoff to be received when the goal is reached.

Let us consider each of these phenomena in turn.

Goals. When we say that people are unmotivated, what we really mean is that they are not deeply committed to the goals that we have selected for them. Certainly anyone who has observed the villagers' dogged commitment in carrying through the legal disputes to protect their land can hardly call them unmotivated in general. The same can be said for the extraordinary and sustained efforts that villagers make to acquire the resources to be spent upon the fiesta of their saint.

These are not the only meaningful goals to the villagers, but they are goals for which the villagers have well established pathways for action and interpersonal relations. For such goals as improvement in agricultural productivity or building a new school, the problem is to convert desires which people have into established pathways of interaction and activity. For this purpose, we must consider the following points.

Anticipated Costs and Rewards. Villagers recognize as well as we do that there is a cost to be paid in the movement toward any goal. In some cases, the cost in money and human effort may be far more than they have been accustomed to put out in maintaining their present level of activities and standard of living. At the very least, the cost will be that of foregoing alternative activities. If the change agent seeks to persuade the villager to plant barley, in effect he has asked him to plant barley on part of his land which has been devoted to corn, potatoes, or other crops. In order to plant the new crop, he is giving up the anticipated rewards that have come from the old.

The costs anticipated may not simply take the form of money and effort. The Indians on the traditional hacienda are beginning to get the idea that through unionization it is possible for them to gain larger money payments, reduced numbers of workdays, and other important improvements in their working relationships. At the same time, they are well aware of the risks involved. They know of cases in the not-too-distant past where an Indian leader, who was trying to rally a community or hacienda population, met sudden death by "accident." They know that they may be put in jail and held there for extended periods of time without the possibility of fair trial. They know that the small plots that they cultivate on the hacienda may be taken away from them. All of these things can happen in the process of building a union organization on the countryside.

They weigh these costs seriously, and they weigh them in relation to the perceived probabilities of reaching their goal, which brings us to the next point.

Perceived Probabilities of Goal Attainment. "The revolution of rising expectations" is often interpreted to mean that people are coming to want things they did not want before. We would argue that the more important aspect is that, as the frequency of communication between backward and advanced areas increases, people are coming to believe more strongly than they ever did before, in the possibility of obtaining certain goals. When we say this, we are referring to the perceived odds of a given outcome. To illustrate the point, let us assume that the members of a given community could be persuaded that, by investing in a certain type of livestock, they could raise their income by 300 percent. Let us assume also that they perceive the odds of this result as being only fifteen in a hundred chances. In this case, if they rejected the innovation, we could hardly say that they were behaving irrationally. (Note further that in this example we have not considered the costs that would presumably be involved in this effort, as discussed above, nor have we considered the time span involved in the payoff, to be considered below.)

What affects the perception of probable odds? A full answer to this question would require a long paper in itself. Let us illustrate with two points that are often overlooked.

The villager does not confront a potential innovation in a vacuum. The new idea comes to him through a particular change agent from outside of the community or is presented to him by a member of the community. Some sort of personal relations are involved, and the villager inevitably tends to evaluate the idea in the context of his past experience in these relations. For example, let us say that the Indian in an indigenous community in Cuzco confronts an agricultural extension agent. The Indian may never have met this particular agent before, but he recognizes him as a mestizo. The Indian and the members of his community have already had a great deal of experience with mestizos, all or nearly all of which has been negative; in fact he feels that he and his fellows have been systematically cheated and exploited by mestizos. Judging in terms of this past experience, it seems quite rational to assume that the odds for a favorable outcome through following the advice of this mestizo are very low indeed.

Many improvements that change agents seek to introduce into the community require cooperative effort among members of the community. If the villager recognizes that the project depends upon good cooperation among villagers for its success, and his experience in the past has led him to believe that poor cooperation is to be ex-

pected, naturally he will conclude that the odds
are against success in this case — however tech-
nically valuable the innovation may be. The level
of trust or mistrust of one's fellow man, therefore,
enters into the estimate of probabilities of success
in working together.

We should also consider the villagers' estimates
of predictability or unpredictability in the behavior of the people on whom they would depend
for the success of the innovation. We have already noted the case where the agricultural agent
explained the use of insecticides but had none
with him to distribute, where the insecticides arrived in the community when the agent wasn't
there to demonstrate their use, and where the
insecticides were misapplied with negative results. We suspect that such cases are frequent
indeed. A new practice must, therefore, be carried out over a period of time through a highly
predictable series of interactions and activities if
a successful outcome is to be achieved. The villagers may quite rationally conclude from their
past experience that this necessary sequence is
not likely to be carried through. Either the
change agent will not be there at some crucial
point when they need him, or the supplies and
equipment will not arrive at the time needed.
Even if they can depend upon the individual
change agent, they may know that this man is
likely to be transferred somewhere else by decisions out of their own control, and they have no

way of judging how well the new man will fit their requirements.

If the perceived odds of success are low, what should be the resultant behavior? We suggest that, regardless of the desirability of the goal, if the odds for reaching it are, let us say, 20 percent or less, then it would be uneconomical and unrealistic to pursue such a goal. In fact, psychologists refer to the tendency to try for "long shots" as gambling behavior, and such gambling behavior seems quite different from the type of risk taking that is thought to be characteristic of people who are striving for economic progress.

Most motivational models, including those that involve level of aspiration or need for achievement, make the prediction that the greatest amount of goal-directed behavior will occur when the odds are at least 50–50. On the other hand, they predict that less goal-directed behavior will be elicited when there is an extremely high probability of the goal being reached, because then the activity will lack challenge. This proposition seems to us probably culturally biased, resting as it does on the assumption that people are highly motivated to accept challenge to begin with. In communities such as those in our study, the task of staying alive is challenging enough so that the villagers are not likely to be seeking further challenges. It therefore seems reasonable to predict that, in peasant communities, there will be little commitment to a given goal unless the perceived probabilities move up toward 100 percent. (We assume that few, if any, changes will be perceived as having a 100 percent payoff probability.) In eliciting goal-directed behavior, in other words, the perceived probability of attaining the goal may be even more important than the perceived value of that goal. A corollary of this is that most things in life are arranged so that, the more important the goal, the lower is the probability of obtaining it. This seems to us a pancultural assumption that may hold up as well in economic development as it does at the race track.

This theoretical point has important practical implications. If change agents concentrate their communications to the villagers upon the high value of the goal to be attained, such efforts may only persuade the villagers that they have a very low probability of attaining it. Activities and communications most likely to elicit behavior directed toward development goals are those designed to raise the perceived probability of reaching such goals.

Anticipated Time Span to Payoff. There is always some gap in time between the investment of efforts and money and the reaping of the payoff, but the magnitude of this time span is of great importance. If people have been accustomed to living in terms of a short time span of several months between planting and harvest, a proposal that would extend the time between effort and payoff to several years requires both a drastic change in the way villagers think about their activities and the world around them, and in their handling of money and credit.

For a people in extreme poverty and with a low level of education, we can assume that it would be foolish to begin an improvement program with a project that has a long time-span payoff. In fact, in the applied anthropology program carried out in the indigenous community of Cuyo Chico, Dr. Oscar Nunez del Prado decided to begin with a work project to improve the homes of the villagers — something whose advantages they could enjoy as soon as they had completed the work. It was only after a number of other such projects had been successfully completed that he got the villagers involved in planting eucalyptus trees. With the irrigation water that they had already provided, the perceived probability of payoff of this project was high, but it also had an exceedingly long time span — fifteen years between planting and harvest. Just as the people of Cuyo Chico accepted this long time span only after a period of development, so the people of Huayopampa decided to shift to planting of fruit trees only after many other developmental changes had taken place.

This problem of anticipated time span creates still others in that, the greater the time span, the more the individual must have confidence in his capacity to control his environment. In most cases of economic underdevelopment we are dealing with a fatalistic culture, where there is little confidence in being able to manipulate the current environment, to say nothing of the future. We are dealing with a culture where (beyond the harvest to planting period) the very concept of storage, for instance, is ill-developed. Concepts of storage and delayed gratification are not readily grasped and acted upon in situations where scarcity prevails.

At this point, we should distinguish between verbalization and commitment to activities. In political systems, large long-range goals are often verbalized; we may even find the peasants themselves talking as if they accepted such goals. Large goals have the appeal of noble purposes, and they conveniently allow for face saving if a project fails; people can tell themselves that they did not really expect it to succeed anyway. But behind the verbal facade, what we actually find is that, not expecting the project to succeed, the people devote little effort to it. Commitment to a goal can more realistically be measured by observing the activities people are willing to commit to it.

Throughout this discussion, we have spoken about the *perception* of costs, of probable odds, and of the time span of payoffs. We speak of perception because it is important to know how the villagers evaluate the world around them, and we must recognize that a given reality as perceived by an observer may not be perceived in the same way by the villagers. Nevertheless, let us not assume that perceptions are entirely shaped by the culture of the villagers or by their particular personalities. There is a connection between reality and perception. It is a fact that eucalyptus trees take fifteen years to grow to maturity, and the villagers of Cuyo Chico perceived this fact. To the villagers, like the rest of us, reality is judged in terms of past experience and, if the past behavior of change agents has been unpredictable, they will anticipate unpredictability from such characters in the future.

INCENTIVES AND SOCIAL ORGANIZATION

Some years ago, sociologists and psychologists were busy trying to prove to the economists that economic man did not exist, that man responded to other than economic influences. This led to much fruitless discussion, mainly for two reasons. In the first place, economists never believed that man responded only to economic influences. They were always prepared to admit that other influences had an impact upon behavior. The problem was that they did not know how to integrate these other influences with the economic, and on this they received very little help from the behavioral scientists. For a long time, anthropologists, sociologists, and psychologists seemed to be trying to prove that economic influences were unimportant, that social and psychological influences weighed more heavily in determining behavior. This, too, proved to be a fruitless enterprise, not only because it reflected a parochial disciplinary view, but also because it bypassed the essential theoretical problem of integrating economic and other variables.

We should all now be prepared to recognize that economic influences are of exceedingly great importance and that there is no point in trying to determine the relative weight of economic and noneconomic influences. Let us, therefore, face the problem of integration of the variables.

Our discussion of economic incentives, agricultural activities, and social organization should provide some guidance along these lines. Here we take it for granted that the individual has some interest in increasing his economic returns, but we also recognize that in the real world there is often no direct connection between a given economic incentive and the pattern of agricultural activities and the social organization through which this incentive is channeled.

It has always been recognized that the size of the potential economic reward is important. Economists have also recognized the importance of risk taking. In our previous discussion on motivation, we noted that the *perceived* probability of gaining the reward must also be taken into consideration. In our discussion of various types of improvement projects, we sought to show that an adequate theory of incentives requires us to consider not only size and probability but also the pattern of activities and the structure of the organization through which they are carried out. Only if the incentive is appropriately linked with these patterns and structures will it serve to stimulate the activities designed for it by change agents. To show further how this theoretical approach may be given practical application, let us consider the modifications we would introduce into the field of community development.

Popular theories of community development lay great emphasis upon such democratic notions as consultation, personal involvement, and decision making by those who are going to carry out the work activity.

Influenced by our U.S. democratic culture and our relatively high level of interpersonal trust, we tend to believe that participation is good in and of itself. While the last word on this concept is yet to be written, research does indicate that one aspect of participation that contributes to the attainment of goals is the degree of commitment that takes place through the process of participation. Quite often such commitment is made publicly. In communities where individuals trust each other and where participation takes place via public discussion, one important meaning of this act of commitment from the point of view of motivation is to increase the probability of attaining a goal by seeing others' commitment —

one feels that he is not the only one who is going to be working for the goal in question. In some communities it is typical for nearly everyone to get up and talk in favor of a project. This may do nothing to raise the perceived probability of attainment if few people believe that the other fellow will actually carry through with his commitment. Thus a low level of interpersonal trust may greatly limit progress where cooperation is required for a project. Participation of a verbal nature in the planning activity may be irrelevant in changing the perceived probabilities and in fact may only play upon the deep suspicion that everybody will talk about it but nobody will do anything about it.

Here we need two clarifying statements: (1) participation should not be regarded as an end in itself; (2) participation is a vague term. In a concrete case, we need to recognize that different work projects require different patterns of interaction and activities and that people's abilities to establish and maintain such patterns will be influenced by the social structure of which they are a part.

The community development literature does not completely neglect community structure, but it tends to deal with structure in terms of informal leadership patterns: the change agent should work with and through the informal leaders. Let us assume that a certain Fulano de Tal, who is opposed to the change agent's development idea, is simply first among his peers, an informal leader, related to his fellows through kinship, friendship, and mutual obligations. In such a case, if the change agent recognizes his position, consults him, and involves him in the planning process, he may be able to win over Fulano de Tal and through him his community.

But suppose the influential Fulano de Tal is a large landowner, who has been enjoying economic and political control over many community members and who has important connections in the capital of his *Departamento* (state). Clearly these two situations pose quite different problems for the community developer. In the latter situation, the involvement-participative approach is not likely to influence Fulano de Tal.

The applicability of a participative strategy will also be affected by the type of project upon which it is to be used. The participative approach rests upon the implicit assumption that those who participate will share in a roughly equal manner in the distribution of the rewards. Absolute equality is neither possible nor necessary, but the perception of gross inequities of payoffs on the part of potential participants will undermine the participation strategy.

According to this logic, where social structural conditions are favorable, the participative strategy can work very well in projects of type 1 (*Individual-Direct*) or type 2 (*Individual through*

Group, with Equal Sharing). But suppose we have a case of type 3 (*The Differential Impact Project*), and suppose our influential Fulano de Tal falls in the group that will suffer an economic loss if the project succeeds? Social participation by itself will not resolve the problem of differential impact, and therefore this type of project is not readily amenable to such an approach.

Let us note the limitations as well as the strengths of our framework. We are far from being able to tell the change agent what to do as he faces varying structural conditions and varying distributions of incentives. For the scientist or for the man of action, we are simply developing a *guide to the diagnosis of community situations* in relation to action programs. A sounder diagnosis should lead both to greater scientific illumination and to more effective action.

A SOCIOECONOMIC THEORY OF EXCHANGE

Economists have long dealt with notions of exchange of goods and services. Sociologists are increasingly coming to think of social life as an exchange process, so one would think that it would now be possible for economists and behavioral scientists to get together.

Let us sketch out the background of exchange theory in sociological thinking. The pioneer in this field was the French sociologist, Marcel

Mauss, with his now classic statement, *Essay on the Gift.*[20] Reviewing all anthropological literature available to him early in the twentieth century, Mauss observed that a principle of reciprocity seems to prevail in human affairs in all tribes and communities. If A gives something to B, B becomes obligated to return the favor at some future time, either in goods or services. While the culture will determine the value of the goods and services that need to be exchanged in order to arrive at a balance, the principle of reciprocity seems to be universal. If B does not reciprocate in the appropriate time period, relationships between the two men tend to break down.

These notions have been adopted and further developed by George C. Homans[21] and Peter Blau[22] in their theories of small group and organizational behavior. Homans and Blau are less concerned with the exchange of economic goods than they are with the balance among such items of human intercourse as personal favors and advice, on the one hand, leading to the manifestation of respect and a feeling of obligation by the recipient, on the other. If B goes to A for advice and A provides the service sought, B becomes obligated to A and may in the future be expected to be more willing than before to do what A asks

---

[20] Glencoe, Ill.: Free Press, 1954.

[21] *Social Behavior: Its Elementary Forms* (New York: Harcourt Brace & World, 1961).

[22] *Exchange and Power in Social Life* (New York: John Wiley, 1964).

him to do. It seems to us that these men provided an open invitation to economists who are interested in integrating their own with other variables, for the theorizing of both Homans and Blau is explicitly based upon such familiar concepts of economics as goods, services, investments, costs, and profits.

We can illustrate this integrated approach to two of the problem areas which we have already discussed. In emphasizing the importance of knowing the cost of the fiesta, we also pointed out that the sponsor generally does not provide all the money or goods for the celebration. He receives help from relatives and close friends. As they give him what he needs, he becomes obligated to them and feels that he must reciprocate in the future. In fact, in literate communities, he keeps a written record of what he has received in order to keep track of his obligations.

Thus we were dealing not only with a specific contribution to the fiesta at a specific point in time but with a series of reciprocating obligations that are built up so that at any one point of time there are a number of incomplete exchanges which must be fulfilled. When undisturbed by outside forces, the reciprocating process can go on forever. The individual is bound into the system and must give what he "owes" when his turn comes. His only escape is to leave the community. This is not unlike the "beholdenness" which ties people together in small New

England villages, and any anthropologist would have considerable trouble explaining certain economic activities at any one point in time, unless he knows something of the history of obligations that have been built up in which specific expectations exist as to who owes whom a favor which must be paid off before alternative activity can be engaged in.

In looking at the network of personal relations that gets village produce to city markets, we sometimes wonder why the farmer consigns his goods to one individual rather than another, where the direct economic bargain seems disadvantageous. Further investigation may show that the trucker does more than just get the goods to the market. Perhaps he also carries messages to relatives and friends of the farmer in the big city. Sometimes he may intervene with a politician or an administrative official in an effort to get some sort of favor for the villager — for instance, the admission of the villager's son into a particular school.

If we are indeed to study the marketing process from the farmer to the consumer in the cities, we cannot afford to limit ourselves to observing and measuring the economic exchanges only. An adequate analysis would have to deal with all the exchanges involved in the process. This approach must also be applied in any intervention that is designed to improve the marketing process from the standpoint of the farmer. If the new marketing process is economically advantageous to him in the immediate handling of his goods but does not provide for the other values that he found in the old system, we can expect that the change agent will have difficulties in carrying through his change. This does not mean that the change agent must guarantee to protect all existing values. It does mean that, unless he is aware of the noneconomic as well as the economic values served currently by the process, his change efforts are likely to be frustrated.

Integration: An Economist's View

While acknowledging the importance of economic factors in rural development, we have been arguing that economists (and non-economists) have not contributed as effectively as they might because they have not been able to link economic and noneconomic variables in their analysis. We have sought to indicate certain ways in which this linking might be accomplished.

We recognize that there are many economists who realize these deficiencies; indeed there are some who are taking the lead in efforts to link economic and noneconomic variables. To review this rapidly developing literature in economics is far beyond the scope of this study. Still, we can point to an intellectual strategy, developed by an economist, which promises to facilitate this linking of variables.

Everett E. Hagen provides such a lead. While Hagen is well known to behavioral scientists through his important book, *On the Theory of Social Change,*[23] the controversy which has surrounded the personality theory he presents in that book has tended to draw attention away from what seems to us his more promising analysis of social structure and social processes.

In a more recent contribution,[24] Hagen makes explicit the social transformations that must accompany economic development. It should be instructive to observe how he does this.

1. He gets down to cases. In "From Bazaar to Store" and "From Cottage Industry to Factory," he examines the economic and social problems involved in the transformation of street vendor to store owner, from artisan to industrial entrepreneur.

2. In both cases, Hagen analyzes how the individual in question would have to organize his activities and his interpersonal relations *if he is to be economically successful* in the more "modern" economic role.

3. Hagen then compares the pattern of interactions and activities *required* for success in the

---

[23] Homewood, Ill.: Dorsey Press, 1962.

[24] "Wealth and the Economy," in Hollis W. Peter, ed., *Comparative Theories of Social Change* (Ann Arbor, Mich.: Foundation for Research on Human Behavior, 1966).

new role with the pattern the artisan or street vendor has carried on successfully in his traditional role.

4. This exploration of the discrepancies between the old and new roles enables Hagen to focus attention simultaneously upon the key social, psychological, and economic factors involved in such transformations.

While we regard his paper as a brilliant contribution to knowledge concerning these important economic and social roles, we find that one of its chief values is its simplicity. Its success does not depend upon his mastery of the theories used by behavioral scientists — although he is extraordinarily well informed on these matters. He does not have to leave his own discipline in order to manipulate the esoteric concepts of other disciplines. He simply examines behavior under two pairs of conditions: the behavior of the street vendor and of the store owner; the behavior of the artisan and the industrial entrepreneur. It is at this basic level of observed behavior that Hagen is able to achieve a linking up of economic, psychological, and social variables. It is on such a foundation that an integrated approach to development research must be built.

Guidelines for Research

The examples from Hagen suggest one essential for progress in interdisciplinary development research: we must get down to cases where behavior can be observed and described. As long as we communicate with each other only in the abstract terms peculiar to our own disciplines, we shall never forge the links in an interdisciplinary theoretical chain. When we talk about behavior in concrete situations and then relate our concepts to that behavior, we shall discover how the concepts of various disciplines can be linked together.

Reflection upon the framework we have presented suggests two further guidelines that have to do with traditional oversimplifications in research and writing about rural development.

Much of our thinking has run in the convenient but misleading dichotomy between *the* city and *the* countryside. To be sure, there are certain properties that cities have in common and that are not found on the countryside, so for some purposes it may be useful to think in terms of city versus country. Unfortunately this style of thinking may trap us into the implicit assumption that, at least within a given country, one rural village is very much like another. We therefore proceed with false confidence to generalize about the properties of villagers.

While this has not been the theme of the present monograph, the illustrations we have used should impress the reader with the great variability that is to be observed within the rural sector of Peruvian economy and society. We have noted the sharp contrast between the coastal commercial hacienda and the traditional sierra hacienda. We have also pointed out the enormous differences between the "captive" mestizo-dominated indigenous villages of our Cuzco area study and the relatively autonomous and self-propelling villages of the Mantaro Valley. We could go on illustrating variability with further cases, but these contrasts should suffice to make the point.

Is Peru unique in the variability to be found on the rural scene? Perhaps, but a prudent scientific view would caution against such an assumption. It seems to us that students of rural development in any country might well assume that a wide range of differences is to be found. The assumption of uniformity will more quickly lead to generalizations, but all but the broadest and emptiest generalizations will then ultimately be proven false. We shall build on a firmer foundation if we look for variability first, and then seek to discover uniformities that will be true of the range of phenomena we study.

Some of the literature on the introduction of change is similarly misleading. Much that has been written seems to be based upon the assumptions that (1) any change is like any other change, (2) men naturally tend to resist change, and (3) that the problem, therefore, is to discover the psychological and social techniques that will allow the change agent to overcome resistance to change.

We have attempted to show not only that changes differ from one another but also that they differ in systematic ways, which present the change agent with distinctively different psychological, social, and economic problems. We have also argued that the social structure of a community has a great deal of bearing upon the process necessary for effecting change.

Only as we take into account differences in community structure and differences in types of change projects will we be able to devise more effective intervention strategies. Finally, those better strategies will depend upon progress in the theoretical integration of economic, technical, social, and psychological variables.

Appendix

Nature of the Current Research Program

As mentioned in the introduction, this monograph grows out of "Study of Change in Peruvian Villages," a comparative and longitudinal research and development program. To place the present publication in context, we present here a brief description of the program.

This is a collaborative program of the School of Industrial and Labor Relations of Cornell University, the Instituto de Estudios Peruanos in Lima, and five Peruvian universities. The principal co-investigators are William F. Whyte and Lawrence K. Williams for Cornell and José Matos Mar for the Instituto de Estudios Peruanos. (Dr. Matos is chairman of the Department of Anthropology of San Marcos National University in Lima.) Associate directors in Peru from 1965 to mid-1967 have been J. Oscar Alers for Cornell and Julio Cotler for the Instituto. Dr. Cotler is continuing in this position; Dr. Alers returned to Cornell for the year 1967-1968, and Dr. Williams is representing this Cornell program in Peru.

Toward an Integrated Theory

The research design and the administrative strategies have been worked out jointly between Cornell and the Instituto in consultation with the participating Peruvian universities. All the research data cited in this report, except as otherwise noted, have been gathered by Peruvian students, working under the supervision of Peruvian professors.

The comparative feature of the program involves study of twenty-six villages in five areas of Peru. In longitudinal terms, this is a survey of these villages in 1964, with plans to apply a similar instrument again in 1969. Through the 1964-1969 period, we are also carrying on social anthropological studies of social structure, political power, and social and economic processes in order to gather data upon the changes we are observing and seeking to measure.

In Peru the villages are being used as continuing field research sites. Students are being trained as they do field work and in short courses and research conferences. Teaching materials are being developed out of the research. At Cornell we have been conducting a seminar devoted to the analysis of our village data (and data from industrial studies in Peru). Several students have used this seminar to prepare themselves for thesis research in Peru or in other Latin American countries.

Data analysis and report writing are carried on simultaneously at Cornell and in Peru. Publications are being issued both in English and Spanish. The first publication, "Proyecto de Estudio de Cambio en Pueblos Peruanos" (Project for the Study of Change in Peruvian Villages) was issued as a bulletin of the Instituto de Estudios Peruanos in 1966 and also circulated as Reprint 9 of Cornell University's Latin American Program. The present volume is being translated for publication by the Instituto de Estudios Peruanos. A monograph in Spanish on the Chancay Valley (including the first six villages surveyed) is in press at this writing.

While the major publications will be area studies examining the 1964 surveys in relation to the social anthropological data and 1964-1969 analyses of changes, we have such a wide variety of human settlements under study that the continuing effort to make sense out of what we see leads us from time to time into the composition of methodological and theoretical statements. The present publication presents a framework which we are using to integrate economic with social and psychological data.

The program has three major purposes:

1. Scientific: to add to knowledge (a) on the process of culture change and economic growth in developing countries, (b) on strategies for the organization of overseas research programs, and (c) on the utilization of research programs for the development of universities overseas.

2. Methodological: to demonstrate how to integrate data from two methods (surveys, interviewing-observation) which are rarely used together and have never to our knowledge been combined on such a large scale.

3. Practical: (a) to contribute to the improvement of the teaching of the behavioral sciences in Peru and in the United States, and (b) to provide information and, when requested, advice on development strategies to agencies (Peruvian, foreign, and international) that are concerned with this field of activity.

The program has had a variety of sources of support. Activities of Cornell have been financed by the Ford Foundation, the Agricultural Development Council, the Wenner Gren Foundation for Anthropological Research, the National Science Foundation, the Advanced Research Projects Agency, the National Institute of Mental Health (Career Research Award for Whyte) and a Fulbright fellowship for Williams. Generous support has also been provided within Cornell by the New York State School of Industrial and Labor Relations and the Latin American Program.

Activities of our Peruvian collaborating individuals and groups have been supported by the Ford Foundation, the Agricultural Development Council, the Wenner Gren Foundation for Anthropological Research, the National Science

Foundation, the Instituto de Estudios Peruanos, San Marcos National University, and, on a somewhat smaller scale, the other collaborating universities.

This book was printed in 11 point Linotype Caledonia at Cayuga Press, Inc., Ithaca, New York.